MEASUREMENTS

OF

BUSINESS

PERFORMANCE

BY

MARTIN GREEN

Table of Contents

Overview

In this work I try to present in some way

clear, accurate, all the facts and theories you need to know,

Understand the importance of corporate performance and the concept of high performance. Note that here the term performance in English prompts us to consider his two terms performance and performance. Additionally, in this work, we take a closer look at some of the methods used by

Management and marketing departments of performance measurement companies (internal performance of the company), as it is very important to exist beyond the qualitative measurement of applicable indicators.

Other criteria for objectively measuring the above concepts.

The aim of this work is the ultimate transparency.

PROLOGUE

In the context of my thesis, which consists of a

gathering information through literature and internet for the search

of the most important Performance or Performance Measurement methods of Business. The amount of information is great as are their needs

businesses trying to survive in a highly competitive environment

environment

This thesis consists of 6 chapters.

In the 1st chapter the definition of performance and performance is analyzed and

what is their necessity in each business/organization.

chapter analyzes the BalanceScorecard method as a tool

Models by Performance Measurement, Prof. Kaplan and Prof. Norton, and BSC proponents and critics.

Chapter 3 refers to KPIs as key performance indicators.

Used for performance monitoring based on business goals.

The chapter analyzes the 6 Sigma method and its objectives.

In the 5th chapter the Total Quality Management system is analyzed, reference is made to its philosophy, its basic principles and structures.

In this chapter, we analyze the indicative benchmarking methodologies.

The definition, its historical background, and its beginnings are mentioned. Then why companies generally use it

The categories of benchmarks, the benefits of applying the benchmarking method, the need to identify errors, and any restrictions on their use should be identified.

INTRODUCTION

Performance indicators are generally quantitative tools that assess a company's performance relative to specific targets or goals

desired result. Key performance indicators can be financial or non-financial in nature. Financial KPIs include investment,

Percentage of revenues and costs to sales from purchasing poor quality goods. All of these examples use numerical information

To measure the performance of commercial organizations or parts thereof (industries, product lines, sales departments, operations, etc.).

Non-financial performance indicators can include the number of times an object occurred or the time it took to occur

Project completed. Examples include the number of customer complaints, the number of orders per day, inspection times, and so on. Such performance indicators are

Performance measurements contain feedback or information about activities performed in that context

supply chain. Its purpose is to assess the achievement of customer expectations and strategic goals. This process results in the identification of specific improvement needs

areas of problematic performance. Using performance counters

Supply chain management plays a key role in evaluating performance, setting goals, and determining future actions.

improvement. On the management side, performance measurements provide decision makers with the information they need to

In charge of procedures. In fact, power measurements show that

help determine their success and potential

Strategies applied, and facilitate their understanding

existing situation. Therefore, accurate performance measurement helps to to intensify the attention of the Administration in matters of revision of the operational ones

objectives and reorganization of business processes.

CHAPTER 1: PERFORMANCE MEASUREMENT

Definition

Performance Measurement

Traditionally, performance measurement is defined as the process quantifying the effectiveness and efficiency of the measured process, system or business1 .

Comment

In modern business management, performance measurement goes beyond the limits of purely quantitative and financial quantities, as it is set the question of how you can manage something you cannot measure.

The measurement of the Performance of a Business was considered by Sink as a complex, difficult, important and often misused process1

, during which they were and have been devised and implemented

many ideas – efforts to be able to measure with the right one possible way. Therefore we see that the given definition is focused in the numbers that management needs to count every time Performance of the whole but also of part of the business.

Performance Measurement

performance counters or key performance indicators

(Key Performance Indicator) is a variable that represents a quantitative evaluation.

Effectiveness and/or Efficiency

2. Any part or all of a process or system related to a standard or goal;

Comment

If we want to see the concept of performance in general, we will understand

that there are no big differences in terms of performance, but to

to measure performance we will also need the measure of performance.

Measuring success refers to the whole **Performance measurement activities3.** Performance measurement is an activity performed by **administrators.**
Achievement of goals set based on strategic **business taxes.**

In this work we will choose the term performance

Is Performance and Performance Measurement Needed?

The objective of performance measurement is to achieve the predetermined

strategy according to qualitative and quantitative specifications, as well

the correct and correct management of resources that are in limitation. This means that basis of the theory of economic problem, in which

we accept that resources are not found in abundance in our environment, but in limitation, then we should check each time how efficiently we can

to manage the resources as a whole so that we can

we achieve the optimal result with the specific resources and to

there is the least possible use of resources, with the most possible combinations for a greater effect4 .

The result obtained from the

measurement is the supply information about efficiency with which the operational resources are converted into outputs and the quality of

the outputs

Elaborating further on the concept of performance measurement will we could say that it is that tool that translates them

strategic goals of the business or organization to specific ones

operational objectives (business objectives) and initiatives that will promote business performance even more dynamically4 . Like everyone

we know the business performance directly depends on its members as well as the planned management exercised by management.

Performance measurement concerns the whole of the organizational systems that create, produce products or provide services,

regardless of character, share compositionand purpose.

Performance Measurement Methods

In this section, we review the definition of performance measurement and then the methods that exist so far in the existing literature.

In fact, the particular subject we are dealing with cannot be adequately defined even by scientists.

It takes multiple efforts to get the right definition, not only in the social sciences but also in economics

concept.

There are many models in the literature similar to those of Norton and Kaplan. These models are designed to measure business performance and link the metrics used to the overall strategy of the business. Below we will summarize the known models used

performance measurement with first always their well-known Balanced scorecard Norton and Kaplan that in fact this model gave the impetus for study

and reflection in the cognitive field of its various measurements business performance and in the development of other and new theories.

CHAPTER 2 BALANCED SCORECARD

General Comments

The Balanced Scorecard (Balanced Measure Table, Balanced Target Table, Balanced Performance Card) is one of them.

A measure of company performance proposed by Kaplan and Norton in 1996. The Balanced Scorecard (BSC) is designed to help organizations with two main goals:

Efficient measurement of corporate performance and effective strategy design.

Modern organizations cannot rely solely on financial numbers to measure their success.

BSC can be described as a set of metrics derived from organizational strategy. These metrics are for illustrative purposes

Organizational progress and performance. Its achievement guides the organization towards the desired goals and overall vision.

The Balanced Scorecard (Balanced Measure Table, Balanced Target Table, Balanced Performance Card) is one of them.

A measure of company performance proposed by Kaplan and Norton in 1996. The Balanced Scorecard (BSC) is designed to help organizations with two main goals:

Efficient measurement of corporate performance and effective strategy design.

Modern organizations cannot rely solely on financial numbers to measure their success.

BSC can be described as a set of metrics derived from organizational strategy. These metrics are for illustrative purposes

Organizational progress and performance. Its achievement guides the organization towards the desired goals and overall vision.

Critical Success Factors (CSFs)

As for the first concept, strategy took on a new meaning in management with the BSC and other PMS developed during 90s, such as VDF (Value Dynamics Framework) .

According to Brewer (2004) the most important step in creation of any PMS is to define the strategy and as Frigo emphasizes (2004), the most successful organizations treat strategy as a continuous process. However, it is also known that many businesses faced various difficulties in order to clearly define the

their strategy (Brewer, 2004, Mintzberg, 1994). In addition, the numbers that presented by Stawar (2002) showed that the strategy is yet another

A very difficult word - 85% of management teams spend less than an hour a month discussing this concept. Weinstein & Castellano (2004) therefore argued that the SMS (Strategic Management System) makes the BSC an important strategic management system.

Ability to provide alternative PMS to overcome deficiencies associated with reliance on traditional financial measurement systems.

Therefore, the BSC was "born" as a PMS but due to the growing importance of the strategy, it was established as SMS. As for the second one concept, i.e. the CSFs, according to Veen-Dirks & Wijn (2002, pp 410)

"can help managers deal effectively with

tensions between strategy implementation and strategy formulation strategy". These two authors argued that CSFs are key "nonfinancial drivers" (nonfinancial drivers) and they should be

key indicators in any PMS in order to express the business strategy. Therefore, in practice a PMS often turns into a

structured version of top management's business vision - the PMS evolves into an SMS, as previously mentioned. Therefore, it can argued that the history of PMS - its inception as a measurement model based on financial indicators and its evolution into multimetric model with an emphasis on non-economic indicators in order to balance them the different and simultaneous dimensions of business - leads to

development of the BSC (and other models) which places more emphasis on strategy and the main functions of the business

The model of Kaplan & Norton

As is well known, the Balanced Scorecard (BSC) was developed by Prof. Kaplan (from Harvard Business School) and Mr. Norton (advisor). In 1996 these two authors developed this model (BSC) based on information technology (IT-based) in order to help the

top-management to choose a set of metrics that provide a

complete picture of the business. Basically, this model indicates the development of four scorecards, one with financial

indicators and the other three with non-economic indicators, as follows:

Perspective)

company's long-term financial goals

• Customer Perspective:

Metric Description

Target group (e.g. customer satisfaction, customer loyalty, etc.)

• Internal Business Process Perspective Categories:

Emphasizing the internal processes necessary to deliver the value expected by all shareholders,

Essentially, the two authors (Kaplan and Norton) recognized some of the weaknesses and ambiguities of his previous PMS. As a result, the BSC-based approach is

A clear prescription of the measures an organization should take to keep the financial dimension from being unbalanced

financial figures. they reasoned this to balance

Between economic and non-economic indicators to consider

What are his 4 categories/dimensions of BSC causally linked and what is not?

Considered individually (synergistic effect). However, the four proposed categories do not limit BSC. number

it depends on the industry in which the business operates and on the strategy

Kaplan & Norton's work with BSC, bridged the gap between development of strategy and its implementation with support and connection

four "critical processes."

management"(critical management processes):

• Clarify and translate the vision and strategy,

• Communicating and linking strategic goals to metrics,

• Enhance strategic feedback and learning.

In addition, the BSC framework (like any other PMS) has priority aimed at providing relevant and balanced information to top management (Mooraj, Oyon & Hostettler, 1999) - management cannot spend

more time analyzing information than making decisions. Against

consequently, the main role of the BSC is to provide the critical information that are used in the decision-making process. Furthermore, these latter authors pointed out that the role of this model depends "on the motivation/reason for developing the BSC and on

which stage of it will be implemented" (Mooraj, Oyon & Hostettler, 1999, pp 482). For example, they pointed out that in Europe many organizations implement BSC with an emphasis on planning rather than control: using the BSC as a tool;

for all managers to start thinking strategically about the organization and his future.

In order to fully understand the appearance of the BSC one must consider the following key issues regarding this model

• Initially, Kaplan's previous work was in cost accounting

company's long-term financial goals

• Customer Perspective:

Metric Description

Target group (e.g. customer satisfaction, customer loyalty, etc.)

• Internal Business Process Perspective Categories:

Emphasizing the internal processes necessary to deliver the value expected by all shareholders,

Essentially, the two authors (Kaplan and Norton) recognized some of the weaknesses and ambiguities of his previous PMS. As a result, the BSC-based approach is

A clear prescription of the measures an organization should take to keep the financial dimension from being unbalanced financial figures. they reasoned this to balance

Between economic and non-economic indicators to consider

What are his 4 categories/dimensions of BSC causally linked and what is not?

Considered individually (synergistic effect). However, the four proposed categories do not limit BSC. internal business processes but

and from the external results (outcomes) in order to improve continuously strategic performance and results. When the BSC fully develops, transforms strategic planning from a

academic exercise in the backbone of the business.

Successful implementation of a strategy requires all employees to align and connect with strategy (Kaplan & Norton, 2001).

The idea of these two authors was to divert top management's attention away from budgets and operations.

Plan ¨ (budget and operational plan) that defines

strategy and CSF, including financials (this is still important)

The goal of BSC, as defined by Mooraj, Oyon, and Hostettler (1999, p. 481), is therefore: ``It should concisely summarize and promote the company's key success factors.

they talk about past events,

industrial enterprises, investing in long-term skills, and

Customer relationships have never been so important to success. But these economic measures are not enough to guide and measure corporate direction.

Toward Realization of the "Knowledge and Information Age"

Future value from investments in customers, suppliers, people, processes, technology and innovation." Furthermore, it is widely recognized that BSC draws on some key concepts from previous theories of corporate governance. B. Total Quality of Management (TQM). As an example of this (according to the website:

www.balancedscorecard.org), BSC includes feedback.

As for the output of internal business processes such as TQM,

Additionally, add a feedback system for the results of your business strategy. This creates a "feedback" process

"Double Loop" (Double Loop Feedback) in BSC.

In addition, another important aspect of the BSC model is the measurement system. According to the website www.balancedscorecard.org, "You can't manage what you can't measure." Therefore, indicators should be developed based on strategic planning priorities. According to Kaplan & Norton (1996), the measurement procedures designed to collect information related to them

metrics that are predetermined according to the strategic plan and to them reduce numerically for storage, presentation and analysis. Thus, the decision makers consider the outcomes of various

Measurable processes and strategies and long-term financial goals of the company

• Customer Perspective:

Indicator description

Target group (e.g. customer satisfaction, customer loyalty, etc.)

• Internal business process perspective categories:

Emphasizing the internal processes necessary to deliver the value expected by all shareholders,

Essentially, the two authors (Kaplan and Norton) recognized some of the weaknesses and ambiguities of his previous PMS. As a result, the BSC-based approach

A clear description of the actions the organization should take to prevent financial imbalances

financial figures. they reasoned this to balance

Between economic and non-economic indicators to consider

Which of the four categories/dimensions of BSC are causal and non-causal?

Viewed individually (synergy). However, his four suggested categories do not limit his BSC.

100% of the Fortune 1000 (higher from the previous survey) of companies have implemented BSC by 2002. Also, Brewer (2004) highlighted that more and more businesses,

large and small, are likely to implement the BSC in the near future.

Also, the work of Kald & Nilsson (2000) showed that by 1999 as much as 27% of companies incorporated in the Nordic stock market,

they used PMS with financial and non-financial indicators in particular

that of the BSC. Also, there was a clear indication that the presentation of the BSC in

conferences and in financial journals contributed enormously to its dissemination.

company's long-term financial goals

• Customer Perspective:

Metric Description

Target group (e.g. customer satisfaction, customer loyalty, etc.)

• Internal Business Process Perspective Categories:

Emphasizing the internal processes necessary to deliver the value expected by all shareholders,

Essentially, the two authors (Kaplan and Norton) recognized some of the weaknesses and ambiguities of his previous PMS. As a result, the BSC-based approach is

A clear prescription of the measures an organization should take to keep the financial dimension from being unbalanced

financial figures. they reasoned this to balance

Between economic and non-economic indicators to consider

What are his 4 categories/dimensions of BSC causally linked and what is not?

Considered individually (synergistic effect). However, the four proposed categories do not limit BSC. traditional techniques of financial criteria

in strategy and mission – in a
mix of a set of dimensions,
technical   and

indicators/metrics, where finance is a part only this.

• Internal business process perspective categories:

Emphasizing the internal processes necessary to deliver the value expected by all shareholders,

Essentially, the two authors (Kaplan and Norton) recognized some of the weaknesses and ambiguities of his previous PMS. As a result, the BSC-based approach

A clear prescription of actions an organization should take to prevent financial imbalances

financial figures. they reasoned this to balance

Between economic and non-economic indicators to consider

Which of the four categories/dimensions of BSC are causal and non-causal?

Viewed individually (synergy). However, his four suggested categories do not limit his BSC. BSC for those who have used it - a fact that recognizes the importance of this model.

From this we can conclude that BSC is the perfect way to gain engagement, at least in theory.

Wars of the BSC

However, the BSC is not immune to criticism. For example, reviews 1999) from the article by Mooraj, Oyon & Hostettler and Maltz, Shenhar & Reilly (2003) showed that this model fails:

,

• To determine the role of existing communities (isolating

individual performance and achievement) and

• To identify a PMS with a two-way process

(in contrast it focuses on the top-down direction)

Therefore, these authors argued that the BSC model "will

judged on whether it is good if it adds value to the organization and will be considered necessary if it proves to be necessary in management" (Mooraj, Oyon & Hostettler, 1999, pp. 481) and "despite the widespread use of the BSC, it is shown to it is inadequate in different circumstances and in different types of companies" (Maltz, Shenhar & Reilly, 2003, pp. 204).

Moreover, Mooraj, Oyon & Hostettler (1999) concluded that the BSC could be a good tool, however many similar ones

systems have recently been developed – tableaux de board (Epstein & Manzoni, 1998), performance prism (Andy Neely, et al, 2002) - thus, the question is "is

is the BSC really necessary?'

Maltz, Shenhar & Reilly (2003) argued that the lack of emphasis on category of human resources (HR) is the main weakness of BSC. They presented the case of the American company "Best Foods" (now part of Unilever) which used this model for a few years and

felt the need to add a fifth category - "Development

of human resources" –. However, it should be mentioned that his work Kaplan & Norton (1996, 2001) did not limit the use of BSC to only 4 categories. Instead, they suggested that Organizations should create their own BSC and add the categories they find.

Some important functions of the company are not possible

Conventionally, he falls into four categories. Therefore, the criticisms of these authors in the original Kaplan and Norton papers could be viewed as unfair.

Moreover, recent criticisms of BSC are based on defining strategies. Veen-Dirks & Wijn (2002)

A study by Prof. David Otley found that the BSC does not provide sufficient feedback on strategy and cannot be used to steer strategy. These authors pointed out serious errors in BSC.

How can I check the logic of the strategy? BSC works perfectly and

However, it is useless because corporate strategy is poorly defined. But the main criticism comes from Danish scholar Anne Norekrit. This author (2003) also BSC

Gets a lot of attention, persuasive rhetoric is more important than persuasion theory – "the question is: the BSC receives so much attention because of of its substance and content or simply because of its promotional rhetoric?"

According to her, the BSC was developed with the intention of convincing the reader for its truth – "represents a drama and creates

a drama, appeals to the audience's emotion and less to reason their".

CHAPTER 3: KPIs (Key Performance Indicators)

General comments

"Key Performance Indicators (KPIs) are important metrics that are used to monitor performance based on them

business goals. KPIs measure improvement or

deterioration in the performance of an activity that plays an important role for her successful operation of a business according to the IBM website http://publib.boulder.ibm.com/infocenter/dmndhelp/v

6r1mx/index.jsp?topic=/com.
ibm.btools.help.modeler.doc/doc/concepts/measures/
kpis.html.

customers is an important business activity. A KPI

it can be the Average response time
to customer calls with target less
than one minute.

KPIs are based on business objectives.
The business person goal is
quantifiable, measurable and oriented
to

result. The goal is converted into a KPI with which the

organization is able to measure some dimension of
the process in terms of target that has been set and
the total of euros. In WebSphere Business Monitor,
the KPI is compared to the target and ranges to
determine the level

of success.

KPI indicators do not refer to a specific
execution of a process but calculated using
data from multiple runs'.

Definition of KPIs

"Key Performance Indicators (KPIs) are important metrics that are used to monitor performance based on them

operational goals. For KPI indicators a target or ranges are specified or both to measure whether the business is achieving its goals.

CHAPTER 4: Method 6 Sigma

General Comments

This is a quality control strategy that allows no more than 3.4 defects per million.

In 1986, Bill Smith, Senior Engineer at Motorola Inc., introduced the concept of 6 Sigma. 6 Sigma provides specific ways to redesign processes or to redesign processes.

So that early flaws and mistakes do not reappear.

That is, it has a preventive nature. Therefore, this methodology is also called best-in-class.

The number of defective products and their wasteful operating costs are reduced, thereby increasing profits and quality

Improve product and customer satisfaction, and increase the profitability of the companies that use it. some distinctive examples

These companies are Motorola Inc. itself.

Ford, Caterpillar, Microsoft, Raytheon, Quest, as well as $17 billion on this innovation, General Electric and more from his $300 million in the first year of implementing 6 sigma

Diagnostics, Seagate Technology, Siemens, Merrill Lynch, Lear, 3M and many more.

Participation of all employees is very important. The company must provide opportunities and incentives for employees to concentrate their talents and abilities to satisfy customers. .

4.3 Statistical Concept of Six Sigma

The term sigma is the Greek letter (ÿ) of the alphabet and is used to describe the standard deviation in statistics

than average. A common metric for 6 Sigma is DPMO (Defects Per Million Opportunities), which can include:

Everything from components, pieces of hardware,

or lines of code, to forms of management, timeframes, or distances. The Sigma quality level indicates how often a defect is expected to occur, with higher Sigma quality levels indicating more defects.

A process that is less prone to error. Against

As a result, as Sigma's quality levels increase, so does the need for less control, reduced costs and increased product reliability.

Increase customer satisfaction. this is

Use the DMAIC (Define, Measure, Analyze, Improvement, Control) methodology. This is a methodology for existing procedures that can accommodate changes for improvement or a DMADV methodology (define, measure, analyze, design

CHAPTER 5 BENCHMARKING

Benchmarking practice is the systematic process

of comparing one's organizational structure, processes and performance organization, with the best practice organizations worldwide,

with the ultimate goal of the specific organization moving towards it business excellence

Definition of Benchmarking

According to the definition of the European Foundation of Quality Management

(EFQM), Benchmarking practice is the systematic process

of comparing one's organizational structure, processes and performance organization, with the organizations showing good practice in

global level, with the aim of the specific organization seeking to move towards business excellence5 . The main goal is improvement

of the business through its comparison with the best competitors, while

at the same time it is given the possibility to:

• To quantify existing differences in performance, if this is strongly the case,

• Document why these differences exist.

• Recognize the steps you need to take to overtake and outperform your best competitors. By the term 'performance' is meant the degree to which executives and businesses achieve their organizational goals with efficiency and effectiveness6 .

From the above we can see that the *benchmarking* technique is not just an attempt to copy the processes and practices of other businesses with excellent performance, but a systematic effort to learn and adapting the best processes, in harmony with the interior

business environment. This technique can be applied to all

almost the operations and supporting processes of a business, while

in recent years there has been a clear tendency for its increased application specific technique, with the main objective being the survival and development of each business in the competitive economy.

Historical Review

The first applications of the benchmarking technique appear early on of the 1880s, when the American sewing machine company Singer

Sewing Machine established the world's first mass production factory and interest moved towards a closer examination of this biomechanics innovation. Many industrialists of that time in the USA, it seemed

eager to learn how they could apply the new technology in their own industry and take advantage of it.

In 1912, Henry Ford, observing the cutting of meat in a slaughterhouse in Chicago, (each worker took turns doing a different job on the carcasses that were passing in front of him), he thought and created in just six months

later, the first industrial serial production line. The innovation his idea, which really revolutionized its field

automotive industry and industrial production in general, did not originate from the environment of the automotive industry, but from a Third production process7 .

In 1980 the Massachusetts Institute of Technology appointed a committee of special experts to examine the situation of the American

industry. The conclusion that emerged from the relevant research was that the most successful businesses still have one thing in common

"the /TT4 12 Emphasis they give to *competitive benchmarking:*

that is, in comparing the performance of their products as well as of processes they use with those of the companies that lead the world in their sector"8

When did Benchmarking start?

Many of the largest and most successful Japanese companies are known for their ability to collect, process and use information about their industry competitors.

who they work for, their products or practices. in spite of everything

Benchmarking as a comprehensive methodology was developed ten years ago.

From the 80's by Rank Xerox. At that time, Rank Xerox was facing increasing competitive pressure in the international market accompanied by a rapid decline in market share.

Financial issues and problems in

controlling overall costs and product quality9.

To address the above disadvantages, the decision was made to design and implement an ambitious benchmark program for almost every function of the company. The

this program involved the comparison of a large number of indicators, including the unit cost of the business against the

main competitors, their quality and other characteristics

products. The whole process started with an in-depth survey of the satisfaction of

consumer and user reaction to Xerox products.

Then an attempt was made to compare the quality of the products and services and business practices with that of major Japanese competitors.

Initially, the main object of analysis was relatively easy to measure dimensions such as cost. Then, and as the executives acquired

greater experience with the method, examination of

practices and

of critical factors that determine whether the various types of costs that is subject to benchmarking it is possible to be affected by the business. The above attempt to apply benchmarking as basic business philosophy resulted in dramatic cost reduction,

with a simultaneous improvement in the quality of the products, as well as the gradual

reducing new product development time. The end result was, in less than a decade, the company regained its market shares in

international markets.

Xerox's experience led it to adopt benchmarking as an enterprise-wide effort that became integral

part of its business culture, in the effort to achieve better

quality and competitive success. Thus, today both Xerox's strategic and operational programs contain benchmarking analyses10 ,

while some of the world's largest companies e.g. Eastman Kodak,

GTE, General Motors, Motorola, AT&T, DuPont, Corning, NYNEX, Ford, have develop their own benchmarking programs.

At this point it is worth noting that apart from businesses, organizations such as government agencies, hospitals and universities have discovered the value of benchmarking and apply it to

improve the processes and systems they use. In addition, in industry space benchmarking techniques are adopted to achieve

improvements in specialized areas, while recently, state agencies have begin to investigate the use of said practices as a tool for

policy implementation processes, with a focus on work contexts that they are under the business environment and the economy in general.11

Reasons for Using Benchmarking

The Chinese general Sun Tzu often claimed that: "if you know well both your opponent and yourself, then you shouldn't you fear the outcome of a hundred battles". This opinion has been important application in the field of business. With a view to achieving it

competitive advantage businesses try to compete with

to the market by offering superior products, reducing production costs, improving quality, adopting more successful strategies, etc.

The main purpose of benchmarking is the 'decryption' of strategies, practices and processes of competitors, the detection of strengths and weaknesses, as well as the use of information

of this for the design of the steps to be followed in order to outdo competitors.

In the event that the above procedure is not followed, h business is driven to a disadvantageous position, unable to adapt to changing, complex and uncertain environment and eventually loses her its competitiveness.

The reasons that contribute to the deterioration of the situation are:

• You lose touch with your customers' real needs, resulting in a weaker business in terms of quality products and customer service.

• Loss of contact with suppliers, reducing the ability to leverage critical ties and partnerships with suppliers on issues related to the quality of the intended product.

and services, order frequency and size, etc.

• Loss of contact with other key stakeholders of the business, such as society, shareholders, etc.

Through Benchmarking many 'problem' businesses were forced out to look for the reasons for their disadvantaged position, to identify them main causes of their lag and then proceed to

restructuring many of their activities with the aim of improving it

quality. At the same time, it became possible to reduce overheads, which

they concealed the great waste of resources and the severe rigidity of adjustment

of the business in the prevailing market conditions. In table 1

the differences and results in the operation of a business with or without the use of benchmarking12 are presented .

Xyyy Benchmarking

In identifying customer needs

• Customer needs are determined based on the experience or intuition of executives, with an uncertain degree of diagnosis of

Using Benchmarking

Customer needs are identified based on objective knowledge of market trends and improved reliability.
• Based on

real

examples. • Increased objectivity and

response. In

correct and

reliability. • Leading the industry with

the effectiveness of the objectives • Lack of focus on external factors with

a tendency to react to changes.

- Lag

adaptation to industry trends.

- Pursuit of marginal changes based on immediate historical

data. In developing appropriate

measures of progress

- Conducting subjective or personal

proactive perspective and action on changes.

• Pursue significant changes based on real third-party

successes. • Dealing with serious

problems. • Understanding genuine desired

outcomes. • Selection of

solutions based on best practices.

• Clear understanding

strengths and weaknesses. • Selection of easy to accept and

implement

solutions. Comparability of actions with

industry practices • Focus on internal issues. • Gradual evolutionary course. • Acceptance of mediocre

Drastic feasible improvements.

•   Search for performance excellence.

•   High degree of commitment to goals. •

Proactive search for better methods. •

Formulating alternatives • Policy

to   outperform   competitors.

of solutions. • Policy of copying competitors.

The necessity of applying Benchmarking techniques is considered imperative for making significant changes and improvements to

processes used and in the goods and services offered, with

aimed at the best response to the customer's requirements. At the same time, study of the competitive strategies of other companies provides significant data for the formulation of the followed strategy. Following

the mentioned development technique, the business fully understands the competitive environment in which it operates and achieves

gaining and maintaining competitive power through its superiority performance and the achievement of quality results. At this point

the creation and integration of an appropriate system is deemed necessary quality assurance.

General Benchmarking Categories

From the first stages of implementing benchmarking practices they have alternative classification systems have been proposed by different analysts

of said techniques. Taking for granted the fact that each category has its own advantages and disadvantages, businesses apply those benchmarking categories that help promote it

broader policy and contribute to the formulation of various and specific ones objectives that in later stages will be translated into individual programs action. The categorization that follows is based on three different criteria and includes eleven benchmarking categories13 .

Having as a categorization criterion *the point of reference to which comparisons and conclusions are based on,* we have the following benchmarking categories:

1. **Internal:**
It includes the application of techniques Benchmarking between internal functions and is one of the

most simple forms of comparison,
as most businesses apply

similar processes in their internal
organization. Object of comparison it is
usually some product, service or some
specific function. The direct benefit
resulting from the application of this
technique is

the recognition of the most efficient practices in
terms of time and cost and h

transferring them to all departments of the company.

At this point it should be mentioned that its exclusive
use

internal benchmarking without combining it with
the benefits of other techniques can be harmful
unless used as a basis for application

external benchmarking in later stages of business
maturity.

2. **Competitor:** Includes
comparison

of specific practices with the corresponding ones they
apply

competitors more effectively, with the aim of
copying them. The comparison this may

include general procedures or services in particular

product design measures, business processes or administrative methods14. Such comparisons are often difficult to complete,

since competitors do not always disclose the key factors, in on which their success rests. For this reason the "competitor benchmarking" is better applied in cases of partnerships or cooperatives, where interested parties exchangeuseful

information and reap the corresponding benefits. At the same time, in order to better results are achieved, an external one can be appointed

representative specialized in the organization of the whole process, with the aim of

gathering useful information and applying brainstorming techniques.

3. **Industry:** Industry benchmarking presents a lot

common elements with competitor benchmarking. The element that differentiates them two categories are that in the first among the compared parts

non-competitors of the company concerned also take part. Thus, the comparison is made on similar measures applied by companies

of the same industry followed by common adoption characteristics, related to technology or market trends. Because

competitors do not take part in the whole process, the participants do willing to share the secrets of their success, while the only problem that can occur is denial

of participation by businesses that have a surplus of relevant data, due to

annual application of benchmarking techniques.

1.   **Gen eric:** We focus on finding best practices regardless of the industry your company belongs to. Contents:

2.   •
Comparison with other organizations to set

strategy

3.   Con
tribute to the improvement
of the organization itself.

4.   •
Identify   and   apply   best
practices

5.   org
anization.

6.   Thr
ough common benchmarks,
companies demonstrate the
prowess   necessary   to
achieve 'best practices' and

7.   Mot
ivate company employees
to pursue ambitions and
innovative   improvement
plans.

8.   2.
global:

9.   Incl
udes   comparisons   to
organizations   with
geographic   locations
outside   the   national

borders where the company in question is home. in this way

10.   Abil
ity for an organization to adopt policies that it uses for other organizations

11.   con
ditions.

12.   sta
ndards,   comparisons, benchmark categories,

13.   is
formed:

1.   **Process:** In this category it takes place

comparison of similar processes in heterogeneous enterprises.

Examples of such procedures are the management of complaints

customers, the advertising campaigns, the receipt and processing of orders, the staff recruitment methods or the methodology followed during strategic planning15. Although it is considered a relatively effective method, it is

difficult to apply as it requires an in-depth understanding of both its entirety process, as well as individual processes. Often in addition to procedures, organizations compare and performance. The main goal is

determining how other organizations achieve efficiency;

superior quality, cost reduction, introduction of improvements and innovations and consequently the improvement of finances results. 2.

Functional (Functional)16: It is an application of the process benchmarking, as it includes the comparison of specific business operations between two or more enterprises of the same industry

sector. Specifically, it concerns the comparative evaluation of the functions, of processes, structures, systems, climate, culture and

efficiency-productivity indicators.

A common feature of functional benchmarking and generic benchmarking is that they produce the highest utility when combined with process benchmarking. And that's because comparing performance metrics and of strategic decisions of very different companies does not yield useful results Results. Studies have shown that a combination is best practice

of the results of the process benchmarking with those of other companies from different industrial sectors (functional benchmarking or generi

benchmarking).

3.   Performance (Performance)17: Facilitates managers in assessment of the competitive strength of the business, through the comparison of products and services provided. The object of the comparison are

pricing terms, quality, speed of service, reliability

of the business and other technical characteristics. Manufacturing industries computers, cars, photocopiers and the like

financial services businesses apply the

performance benchmarking as an established and very useful tool.

4. **trategic**
(Strategic)14: It concerns the comparison of the basics of the firm's strategies with those used by competitors and

the recognition of the main changes that should be adopted in order to come up with a successful and effective strategy.

The main questions to be asked are:

• Which market segments are competitors focusing on?

• What kind of strategies competitors are applying in the various segments

of the market;

• What are the competitors' investment policies?

• In which functions are their strong and weak points found competitors?

Once the answers to the above questions are found,

company has the ability to identify the main elements of strategies of competitors who contribute more to achieving higher returns. Benchmarking often brings to light elements of competitors that have escaped the attention of the business.

Finally, with *the purpose of the process as a criterion,* benchmarking categorized into:

1.   Competitive (Competitive)18: Includes the comparison of processes, products and services with those of competitors, with aiming to improve to become a leader in the industry, or at worst opportunity to overtake competitors. It is the most difficult in terms of the application category benchmarking, as competitors usually do not they are willing to reveal the secrets of their success. So, thecollection

information is particularly difficult and time-consuming and requires careful analysis to draw the correct conclusions.

2.   Collaborative   16: Collaborative benchmarking does not have competitive nature such as competitive benchmarking and aims to creating a climate of cooperation for common benefit. A business group exchange knowledge and information about a specific activity with aim for all participants to learn something new. He often takes part

a third party that helps coordinate, collect and distribute data.

Having mentioned the main categories of benchmarking, you should emphasized that businesses need to take some measures for the selection of practices to follow. Specifically, you need to

factor in key factors such as how dependent they are on others businesses, the number of organizations participating in the application benchmarking techniques, the existence of a climate of trust, as well as decisions of strategic importance that affect final decisions.

Benefits from the application of the Benchmarking19 method

Companies that have participated in applying the benchmarking methodology have identified many benefits for both the company and its employees. the most important teeth:

• Identifying the most effective activities and processes

It is considered essential for business development.

• Better and faster responsiveness on the rise

customer demands.

• Implementing more efficient marketing.

• Establish and support strategy, specific and credible goals. • Improved support management.

• Improved and accelerated decision-making process.

• Better competitiveness.

• Achieving performance advantages.

• Organizational change methodologies and ways to inspire them. Human factors that can contribute to the creation of organizations.

A new way of thinking for all employees at all levels,

The ultimate goal is to introduce improvements. In addition, the main benefits that a company can get from it

A comparative analysis of our performance compared to our main competitors includes:20:

Implementing an effective quality assurance system. ÿ Accelerate service speed.

Process improvement.

Definition of internal performance indicators.

Efficient resource management. ÿ Change in management style by senior management.

Requirements for successful benchmarking

Systematic efforts to improve or increase qualitative competitiveness must meet certain conditions.

So that affiliated companies can get more profit

advantage. When applying the benchmark method,

These conditions are:

• some level of support for the program by top management;

Everyone will notice you, both inside and outside the company.

• Active participation and appropriate training of the staff of the Member responsible for the activity.

Included in the benchmark.

• A program focused on meeting needs as completely as possible

Customers. • Using benchmarking techniques to improve competitiveness

Introduction of priorities and improvements.

• Align the benchmark project with an objective strategy (a critical, high-return business problem that aligns with that strategy and corporate values).

• Set realistic and objective goals.

• Selection of the best partners for benchmarking.

• Adequate resources are available, especially in the form of time, money and necessary materials. • Adherence to rigorous processes (design, analysis, implementation, and review).

• Continued and significant efforts to foster mindsets among employees that enable continuous improvement for better customer satisfaction.

• Understanding the company culture to make the

necessary changes in the most appropriate way.

• Commitment to implement necessary changes.

• Using appropriate methods to measure success.

Need to recognize common "mistakes" in its use Benchmarking

Aiming at the best possible utilization of the technique benchmarking, top management is required to know not only the more important benefits arising from its application, but also the

existence of specific "mistakes" that are obstacles to achieving optimal results. The most common mistakes are the following21:

• *Irrational alignment of benchmarking techniques with strategy of the business.* It is often seen being chosen as an object benchmarking a topic that is not related or comes in total opposed to some other priority set by

business. At this point the responsibility rests with the relevant team to conduct the benchmarking process, which must

takes appropriate measures to
prevent or correct related situations.

• *When the concept of benchmarking is confused with participation in a survey.* The application of benchmarking presupposes the evaluation of a active process, which exists for a specific period of time

interval, capable of having clear data on the

its effectiveness and its resources.
When a business starts implementing a
new process, for example creating

quality assurance manual by collecting corresponding manuals

other companies, then it is not about benchmarking, but about research.

• *When the effort to achieve customer satisfaction is ignored.*

There are countless business cases where using them

benchmarking techniques, became so inelastic in the cost of providing them

of their product or service, which they failed to consider

the demands of the buying public, with the end result

that they lose

significant part of the market share. In general, it is preferable to management to follow a balanced approach during development metrics in benchmarking.

- *When benchmarkers seek to identify and*

leverage pre-existing measurements. Every business is not logical

to expect that she can compare her performance with predetermined ones

standards. There are many elements that differentiate it from the other companies, such as the difference in its corporate culture,

of the customers, the segment of the market in which it operates or

of its available resources. The most successful comparison is ensured when after the benchmarking partners have been selected,

an effort is made to achieve similar performance.

- *When the process that has been selected as the object of benchmarking is too large and complex to implement easily.* Every system consists of a set of processes, while each process is one

set of specific tasks. In general, it is preferable to

the comparison of competitiveness indicators across the whole is avoided system, as implementation is extremely costly and time-consuming.

The most effective approach is to select one or more representative processes, analyze them, and use them as templates for your sentences.

Processes for the rest of the system.

• Selection of intangible and hard-to-measure objects. These are often targeted as benchmark problems that are initially very difficult to measure.

For example, "employee communication" is one of the most sensitive issues that exist in a company. If

Proper measurement is required and a team is in place to do this

A benchmark for selecting possible parts of a wider topic

Observe and measure memos in the company's distribution process. • Inadequate behavioral benchmarks

Compare. Application of the benchmarking method assumes that

Interested companies are aware of the characteristics of their internal processes, mainly through systematic and thorough analysis. Data from relevant surveys are the key information provided

Company provides to Benchmark Partner Company in exchange for information requested by Benchmark Partner Company. Based on the above, we need this before approaching a candidate

Our partner, the team responsible for benchmarking, decided what data to extract.

• A benchmark partner company was not selected after extensive research. Choosing the right partner

Very important to avoid lengthy procedures.

Common practice is not to ask partners what they can identify from research references or transferable sources.

• There are no codes of conduct or agreements between benchmark partners. american center

Productivity (American Productivity and Quality Center) provides easy-to-use sample code for benchmarking. teeth

Partners know what they want to learn from each other, how relevant administrative information is performed, who has access to it, and for what purposes data from relevant research will be used is important.

Need to recognize restrictions on its use

Benchmarking

In order to avoid the above common "mistakes" when applying the benchmarking methodology, members of management should be aware of some very important limitations.

They result from the use of benchmarks and are related to the following factors22:

• Company size and level of performance already achieved.

• The need to understand the systematic relationships that occur in the network of all processes within the enterprise.

• Introduction of innovations and improvements in current procedures;

Gain a competitive advantage.

His 1992 study by international consulting firm Ernst and Young identified two of the most important factors influencing the suitability of benchmarks for achieving business excellence.

The first factor is company size, which benchmark studies show is easier to use than technology

Introduction of improvements focused on large companies. Convenience lies in the fact that large companies can hire specialized personnel,

Can perform effective analyzes and formulate them in a meaningful way

Suggestions provided through the application of benchmarking techniques.

The second factor, he said, had to do with the performance of already successful companies, and research showed that companies that were already more competitive were easier to develop.

Align with industry best practices.

A third factor that requires special attention

A systematic connection in a network of business processes serves as a benchmark. The business process is

Points most frequently referenced by interested companies

Introduction of improvements. In this particular case, it is common to select the processes that are considered the most important in the industry and compare them with the corresponding business processes.

High performance and usually uncompetitive. After gathering the necessary elements, identify critical performance "gaps" and plan based on these "gaps".

An action program whose main purpose is to introduce changes to achieve better performance. Dangerous trap at this point

The Benchmark Working Group omits how the selected improvement process connects and interacts with other processes. This is the same as for the organic whole. In this particular case there is no observed gap in process performance

Demonstrate appropriate interventions to

increase competitiveness.

A fourth very important factor to evaluate

This is the maturity stage of the company in order for the comparison to be meaningful. Extensive research shows that benchmarking techniques perform better when the context and method of application are taken into account.

business activity is stable. this situation applies to a greater extent for large and successful enterprises, where the highest management has made significant investments over long periods of time intervals, has been driven to high levels of profitability and has achieved general recognition for her successes. In this case, usually

drastic changes are discouraged, while the implementation of small ones is encouraged

improvements to existing products and processes. According to developments of recent years, the revolutionary changes shaping the new

economy and the introduction of innovative measures start from small and businesses unknown to the wider business world. The innovative ones companies often introduce revolutionary changes in an industry, they contribute in the creation of new markets, determine new conditions of competition and they have the potential to irreversibly change the economic field.

The example of the representative companies in

PC, IBM and DEC, when a small company, Apple Computers, which

founded by two visionaries, Steve Jobs and Steve Wosniac, influenced with the innovations in the way of competition. The same phenomenon happened to others branches of the economy, such as that of steel, where small and new

businesses with innovations led to the decline of large, traditional and successful businesses that had remained fixated on the outdated

way of thinking.

CHAPTER 6: TOTAL QUALITY MANAGEMENT

Basic Principles of Total Quality Management

Our total quality philosophy is based on three structural principles:

1. Focus on the satisfaction of our customers and all stakeholders (managers, employees, suppliers).

2. We value teamwork with everyone participating.

3. Focus on processes aimed at continuous improvement and learning.

At Total Quality, the organization actively identifies customer needs and expectations, integrates quality into production processes, and seeks to maximize its experience and knowledge.

At the same time, it calls for continuous improvement in the organization's overall operations31.

• Customer and stakeholder focus:

to do so

To provide customers with products and services that not only meet their requirements but exceed their expectations, organizations must identify the attributes of their products that add value to their customers and lead to satisfaction and commitment.

• Participation and Teamwork:

Involvement of employees at all levels in decision-making and resolution

Each of the problems in reducing failure with employee motivation and the main means of self-management

value-added activities. A working group was formed to

The goal is excellent cooperation and coordination of all grade departments. This collaboration includes vertical and

And in the horizontal structure of the organization

• Focus on process:

A process is a set of activities to achieve a goal. The goal of every process within an organization should be how the organization creates

value for the customer. The series of processes that take place should be emphasized, not just the production.

THE END